lot

T0170668

Caitlin Press Inc.
3375 Ponderosa Way
Qualicum Beach, BC V9K 2J8
www.caitlin-press.com

Text design by Vici Johnstone
Cover design by Briar Craig
Printed in Canada

Caitlin Press Inc. acknowledges financial support from the Government of Canada and the Canada Council for the Arts, and the Province of British Columbia through the British Columbia Arts Council and the Book Publisher's Tax Credit.

Library and Archives Canada Cataloguing in Publication

Lot : poems / by Sarah de Leeuw.
De Leeuw, Sarah, author.

Canadiana 2021031477X | ISBN 9781773860763 (softcover)
LCGFT: Poetry.

LCC PS8607.E2352 L68 2022 | DDC C811/.6—dc23

# lot

Sarah de Leeuw

CAITLIN PRESS 2022

"How do we talk about the history of this land? How do we talk about the ruptures of colonization? How do we talk about naming, un-naming, and re-naming? How do we talk about the violences of language? Sarah de Leeuw's *Lot* engages with all of these questions through a long poem that drifts through language in the sense that it refuses capture and containment. To draw a line around what this work is would do a disservice to de Leeuw's project of exploding boundaries. *Lot* is about existing in relation to land and place. *Lot* is about resilience and hope. *Lot* is essential."

—Jordan Abel, author of *NISHGA, Injun,* and *The Place of Scraps*

"Tracing—and as often forging or divining—paths through documents, intimacies, and form itself. Sarah de Leeuw's exquisite *Lot* names and unfurls some profoundly detailed psychic maps, ones bundled around Haida Gwaii, the archipelago that comprises her home islands, the ones formerly known as the Queen Charlottes. *Lot* breaks down the hulking shapes and terms of familiar concepts—arrival, race, contact, etc.—to reveal the overlappings of inner harbours and the shapes that learning itself assumes. The repeating chorus of the book—'Lot of my future,/ what I have yet to know'—dances in its ambiguity. The specificity of that lot changes places in different mouths here and the mouths the poem opens—some in wonder, some to devour, some to casually acknowledge the teachings of supernatural beings—make this book a document that strays beautifully and, in so doing, marks the edges of many circles, as another poet said. Fellow reader, Sarah de Leeuw's writing brings terms to terms—one re-encounters words such as that *have* (in 'have yet to know') with its intricate possessiveness and its imperative edge; and one feels the uncomfortable white space as she advises to 'be careful of boats that carry unknown gifts.' And—relatedly—there's the direct address of 'I am copper and a bullet/ and a book and I am/ all that I pretend is not me.' *Lot* is a startling and demanding and beautiful book."

—C.S. Giscombe, author of *Prairie Style*

"When I think 'poetic voice', I think about transforming, informing and transcending from the obvious to equivocal. Sarah de Leeuw's poetic voice does this and so much more in her new collection of poetry, *Lot*. It is 'light and dark;' it is 'intellectually, and moral(ly) superior to any others.' The command de Leeuw has with poetic language and insight is astounding. This book is 'bones and star solid' starkly honouring one of Canada's treasures—Haida Gwaii. Read it! And you will see."

—Garry Gottfriedson, Secwepemc poet, author of *Glass Tepee*, *Whiskey Bullets*, *Skin Like Mine*, and *Clinging to the Bone*

Kung Jaadee hin.uu Xaad kihlgaa dii kya.ang. My cousin Crystal Robinson gave me my name at the memorial potlatch honouring my great uncle, who was hereditary chief of my clan. Yaguu'laanaas sduu dii isgaagang. Kaads Nee sduu dii isgaagang. Dii.uu Gaw Xaadaagang, waagyaan I am also Tlingit, Musqueam, Hawaiian, and I am connected to the Tseilwatuth First Nation through the George family.

Lot. Gam dii guu 'la.anggang. I saw a quote while I was reading Lot: "Daily reminder that colonialism was not a historical event, it is an ongoing genocide." Lot is good for settlers who don't know about colonial violence in BC, and in Canada; it brings up racism early [and] addresses it when describe[ing] Haida Gwaii and things de Leeuw has learned. From the way she [tells] parts of the story, de Leeuw has a strong interest in learning about Haida culture: Lot describes Haida Gwaii and things de Leeuw has learned, in particular [about] traditional foods, and learning haw'aa and chinay. Lot [also] follows [what] John R Swanton was told by Haida ancestors.

I was re-traumatized upon reading Lot, and to let you all know; my trauma isn't to be put on display for all to see, or to enjoy, or even to be entertainment. The stereotypes [written about in Lot] are what I have heard countless times since I was 5 years old. I was bullied by 17 students in my Kindergarten class, when our teacher left the room. Those Armed Force kids told me who I was (at least according to what they thought I was; told to them by their parents, and the parents were told by their superiors; before they were posted to my community of Tlagaa Gawtlaas, or New Masset, on the northern end of Haida Gwaii). I learned to hate myself for most of my life. I learned to love myself on my own, despite the hatred I've felt from countless non-Indigenous people. I am, and I always have been, a human being. I am a human being who struggled with reading Lot.

Colonialism hurts all of us, as we are all part of this web, one world. We are all part of it, and what one does to one affects us all. I believe people interested in learning more about Haida Gwaii will enjoy reading *Lot*. I grew to enjoy de Leeuw's book as well; the descriptions of my home territory reminded me of how much I love the beaches, the fish, the whales. I do not speak of stereotypes as I don't wish to give power to such negativity. Instead, I share the opposite of stereotypes.

I teach people to love themselves, and to love others.

I love myself, and I always will.

—Kung Jaadee, Haida and Squamish Storyteller

*In memory of my friend Ya'Ya Heit.*

*For Margo Greenwood. And almost 25 years of working together against coloniality.*

Early on.
I learn.

The world.
Began here.

Begins.
Here.

In the beginning
this land was

nothing
but

sea water
so they say.

In the beginning
it was both

light and dark
so they say.[1]

Contagion
monsters

are always in-
visible or sporting

beautiful
masks.

There are many names for
land is only one.

There are many names for
water is only one.

There are many names for
light is only one.

There are many names for
raven is only one.

For ocean is only one.
For bear is only one.

For moss is only one.
For berry is only one.

For salal is only one.
For deer is only one.

For salmon is only one.
For river is only one.

There are many names for
stone is only one.

There are many names for
island is only one.

There are many names for
queen is only one.

There are many names for
song is only one.

There are many names for
home is only one.

V0T 1R0
Pop. 282 (2016)

Est. 1907
Elvt. 5m/16ft

557 4149
P.O. Box 19

Hwy. 16
Area: 13.59km$^2$

V0T 1S0
Pop. 852 (2016)

Incorp/ed. 2005
559 6121

Area: 37.28km$^2$
Elvt. 20m/65.25ft

P.O. Box 129
2$^{nd}$ Avenue

No. 2 Reserve
Yagan (No. 3) 86 acres

About No. 5, about 9
No. 6, Ain, 164 acres

About 100 acres
Nos. 2, 3 or 4?

No. 7 (Yan)
Meagewan, No. 8

No. 9, Kose
Reserve #9?

No. 10
27 acres

20 acres
#8 there?

Kung, No. 11
10 or 15

No. 12
No. 13, Yatze

45 acres
No. 12

No. 14 – Jalun
No. 15, 101 acres

About 6 or 8
101 acres

No. 15, Tatense
Otter, $14 each

and the marten $7
Exhibit "D8"

Lots 1546 and 1547
Nos. 8256 and 8257

Lot 1626
Timber Licence No. 37108

7 3/4 acres
Timber Licence No. 2517

Coal licences
Nos. 7965 and 7992[2]

Form a line
from first word to last.

Form a line
from right to wrong.

Form a line
from left to right.

Form a line
from start to end.

From dark to light.
From damp to dry.

Form a line
from one to none.

From grace to terror.
From wing to tip.

From fish to seal.
From a to z.

From water to stone.
From east to west.

From south to north.
From largest to smallest.

Form a line
from youngest to oldest.

From sky to ground.
From root to crown.

Form a line
from night to horizon.

Form a line
from moon to shell.

Form a line
from birth to death.

Form a line
from you to me.

Form a line
from time to time.

From sap to drought.
From plenty to nothing.

From sand to grass.
From fur to pelt.

Form a line
from now to then.

Form a line
from us to them.

Form a line
from outside to in.

Form a line
from spoken to written.

Form a line
from frog to egg.

From heart to head.
From number to sadness.

From blue to map.
From song to moss.

Form a line
from bullet to skin.

Form a line
from ship to fingertip.

Form a line
from end to start.

Beginning word. Sea
water word. Say

nothing but word
word. Land word.

Ground word.
Rain word.

Light word.
Dark word.

Word they say,
world, word.

\*

We are on water.
We land.

We are
on land.

My mother.
My sister.

I step off.
The *Queen*

*of the North*.
There.

Here.
July 1980.

Another ship.
Always we

are arriving
by ship.

A word inside
a world.

Inside a world
a word.

Inside a world inside
a world.

Part of the stories
were told by Isaac,

an old man of
Those-born-at-Lielan.

So far as they go,
the stories are fairly

trustworthy, but many
of them he evidently

knew only in
a very sketchy way.[3]

In 1776[4] Captain Cook landed.
He was unable to define an island.

He did not claim the country
for the British crown. Nor

did he name it. In 1787
Captain Dixon took possession

in the name of King George
and called it Queen Charlotte Islands.

There they lie, waste, fallow
and yet marvellously productive.

As we are told by Francis Poole
the only educated Englishman

who has ever lived
on the Queen Charlotte Islands.

He had no government protection
against the hostility of the natives.

The coast of Skincuttle
is very beautiful.

Cedars huge and venerable. Pines
stalwart and yet everlastingly young.

A perfect tempest from the surface
of waves; locals call it *spoondrift*.

The white party were well
received among the kindly islanders.

A curious kind of savages
given to thieving and liquor

but not devoid of intelligence
fond of forms and ceremonies.

They have an extraordinary
veneration for writing.

Any old bundle of waste-paper
If only there are written characters

upon it. It is precious
and sacred in their eyes.

These savages, though they live
more in their canoes than on land

were quite astonished when
they saw white men swim.

The chief swore eternal
friendship and his daughter

visited them to caution
against a bear. In search

the bear was not found.
He shot a crow

to the horror of the natives
who firmly maintain

their descent from that bird.
It was a very dull life.

Sitting around the log-house
fire, telling stories.

A satisfactory report
on the prospects of copper.

The natives took an interest in proving
their capacity for civilization.

Especially telegraphy filled
them with astonishment.

They held up their hands.
"Powerful is the white man,

wise and powerful." They
need to be continuously

guided, watched,
and controlled.

They generally evidenced
an intelligence far

in advance of illiterate
white men in England.

The heavens were lit up
with streaming splendour.

The sun began to sink
to the westward. A curved

line running along the far east
from north to south.

Fit barriers to
mark an empire.

The impressions made
by Mr. Poole's narratives

is altogether favourable.
The natives are physically

intellectually, and morally
superior to any others

of the North Pacific tribes.
They are quite exceptionally

well disposed toward white men.
They have some vague notions

of a religion, of a Great Spirit
and a future life. They are not

cruel or revengeful
and are not vicious

except that, like all Indians
they are inveterate gamblers.

They have a sad
kind of native music.

They cook their food.
They keep many festivals

but the celebrations
are certainly not "orgies."

The women are decidedly
good looking. Both sexes

have naturally fair
complexions, the "black"

in their cases
being entirely artificial.[5]

Some suspect Queen Charlotte
wife of King George III

who bore the king
fifteen children

was of African descent.
Valdes heard stories

from his Jamaican nanny.
Sir Walter Scott wrote

of Queen Charlotte
she was ill-coloured

her family a bunch
of ill-coloured orangutans.

Her nose is too wide
her lips too thick.

To Baron Christian
Friedrich Stockmar

Queen Charlotte was
small and crooked

with a true mulatto face.
She was seventeen

and a German princess
when she married George.

He met Charlotte for
the first time on their

wedding day, September
8th, 1761. She threw

herself at his feet, he raised
her up, they embraced.

She died in 1818. In 2017
a palace spokesperson

did not deny Queen
Charlotte's African

ancestry. Stating instead
it's a matter of history

and frankly we've got
far more important

things to
talk about.[6]

i.
McKenna-McBride Testimonies
Queen Charlotte Agency

At Massett, B.C. September 9, 1913
Memo by Chairman.

_____ sworn as Interpreter.
The Chairman replied, as follows:

The Commissioners are very
much obliged for the address

which you have just presented
and for the kind way

in which you have received us.
We trust with you

that our work may be
satisfactory all round,

not only to the Indians
but to the governments

which we represent,
and that it may be the means

of bringing increased happiness
and prosperity to the Indians.

ii.
Chief Councillor

_____.

While the entire band here,
numbering 300,

have only 2000 acres
between them.

iii.
Who was it wrote
a letter to me?

iv.
These Haidas were away
at different places at the time

when Judge O'Reilly came here;
he came in the fishing season

when most of their people
were away and the few old

people who were here probably
did not understand what

the commissioners
were saying.

v.
In the old days the Haidas
were amongst the bravest

of brave Indians and had
a name which struck terror

into the hearts of
the neighbouring tribes.

Now you see them a quiet
peaceful, law-abiding intelligent

community. I am sorry
to say that many of the brave

old men have passed away
and lie in a silent tomb.

vi.
We wish to get
some information

with respect to
these Reserves,

who will
testify?

The Indian Agent
knows the character

of these reserves
in full.

vii.
50 frame dwellings,
1 log, 10 shanties,

3 barns, 3 horse stables,
1 milk house,

1 church,
1 school,

1 parsonage,
Agents office

and Residence,
school teacher's

residence and
adjoining barns.

viii.
While we are speaking
of their cattle I should

like to say that the Indians
have a strong complaint

about their cattle
being destroyed

by white men
who shoot them.

Q. Is that a general practice
of the white men here?

A. Well, it seems
to be becoming so.

Q. Who is it that
shoots them?

A. We don't know
who it is. Two

were found a few
Sundays ago

deliberately shot
and left on the Reserve.

Are these cattle shot for
the purpose of getting Beef?

A. I don't think so.
Q. Well do they shoot

them just for sport
or from motives

of malice?
A.  For "Sport" I think.

ix.
Q.  Could you give us
the heads of families,

that is all the males
over 18 and all widow

women, and all
groups of orphans.

A.  The Departmental Statistics
are all that I could give.

I have a book
in the office

giving the ages
of all the different Indians.

Q.  What has been
the tendency during

the last five years to
increase or to decrease?

A.  With this band it
has been about equal.

The same number of births
and deaths.

Q. That is your observation,
that they have about

held their own?
A. Yes.

x.
That it is not
Crown Granted?

It is an old Indian
settlement. Several

of the Indians here
have their gardens there.

There are evidences
of old houses

and the Indians
claim that there

are bodies
buried there.

xi.
The Indian Agent, next
went on to say:

The Massett Indian Reserve
is not all owned by the Massett Indians.

About 12 acres are owned
by the Church people

and 9 acres by the Hudson's Bay
Company. We are on the Church

property now. Mr. Harrison
took it up when he was a Missionary

here, and he managed to dispose
of it in some way to the Church people.

xii.
The Indian Agent stated
that these are matters

which have caused
a great deal of trouble,

as they have led
the Indians to believe

that they have certain
rights in the Country,

which they have
not got.

xiii.
The Indians don't understand
by what right the Church

people and the Hudson's
Bay Company have

got these titles.
Q. Don't they

want the Church
here then?[7]

On evergiven tides rollride
in the visiting visitors, visitor

eyes visitor hair, visitor cells
fingers legs names and nails.

Evergiven are those visitors
bringing evergiving gifts.

Visitor walks and visitor talks
everygiving visitor voices

giving evernames to evervisitors
tiny or giant visitors, visitorsoldiers

visitorwives and visitorbooks.
Where once wind and water

shore cedar salmon sand
were evergiving giving visits

of visit after visit after visit
from day moon slips

to sun ice, light would visit
as evergiving visitor's gifts

the tide rolling in visitors
of evergiving visits are evergiven

visitors, visiting not warmth
not fond or fern or finding found

but an evergiving faith
by the evergiven visitor.

Focus on
quiet targets.

Targets unlikely
to emit utterances.

Cedar trees.
Salmon runs.

Winter cashes.
Clam beds.

Take down
tenacious targets.

Targets standing
in the way.

Language.
Art.

Land.
Kinship.

Aim at
soft targets.

Targets likely
to fold quickly.

Cells.
Children.

Stories.
Words.

Blankets.
Loved ones.

By comparison
words are small.

By comparison
words are very small.

By comparison
words offer little.

By comparison
I have nothing to say.

By comparison
words are very small.

By comparison
not much can be said.

By comparison
what is left to say?

By comparison
words are small.

By comparison
words offer very little.

By comparison
there may be nothing left

to say. By comparison
words are very small.

Wordless
Silence

Wordless
Sea

Wordless
Sky

Wordless
Stone

Wordless
Shore

Wordless
Salmon

Wordless
Splintering

Wordless
Stars

Wordless
Sand

Wordless
Split

Wordless
Spring

Wordless
Sapling

Wordless
Sound

as in       to cast
as in       to draw

as in       an act of divination
as in       a curse or spell  ·

as in       a game of chance
as in       a portion, a share

as in       a person's destiny
as in       rare

as in       royalty paid to mine owner, ore
as in       forming part of a larger whole

as in       person regarded as having a special quality (bad lot)
as in       plot of land

as in       front of a house
as in       small enclosure

as in       site of film studio
as in       a number, amount

as in       very much, with modifier 'a'
as in       allocate, appoint

as in       Charlotte, diminutive of Charles.
as in       Lottie. Oh Lot.

Richard is not
an old man.

But one
of my principal

reasons for consulting
him was that he is

the sole survivor
of his family in Masset. [8]

Lot of my future,
what I have yet to know.

(Re)namings. Queen.
Charlotte.

Haida.
Gwaii.

So many.
New words.

Unsettle.
Rewild.

Lot of my future,
what I have yet to know.

i.
Queen City September 15th 1913.
With respect to Skidegate Indian Reserves.

What is the population of the tribe?
On March 31st this year it was 232.

Q. How many houses
have the Indians at Skidegate?

A.   66 dwelling houses
and 10 shanties.

DR. McKENNA: How do you
distinguish between

a dwelling house
and a shanty?

Q.  Some of the houses
are well furnished

with good serviceable
modern furniture?

A.  Yes, far better
than the average Indian home.

What is the character of the land there?
Rocky.

As to the other you cannot speak?
Only from complaints of the Indians.

And what do you mean by that?
They have complained ... of people

destroying the houses by pulling
them down and using them for

firewood. The people claim their
houses have been destroyed by whites?

Yes. Do they trap to any extent?
Do they do any handlogging?

You were not Indian Agent
at the time the mill was working?

Yes, I was, but they employed
Japs principally.

Owned by a company.
A company of Indians?

Do you mean to say that the
share-holders are principally Indians?

ii.
They complained white men
were fishing in the River

contrary to regulations.
Q. In what respect

were they breaking regulations?
A. They were fishing for salmon

inside the river limits.
Q. Did you make any

further applications for additional
lands for the Indians?

A. No.
Q. For what reason?

A. The Indians would not
tell me what they wanted.

Q. Do you think they have enough land?
A. No, I do not think they have enough land.

iii.
How does the Birth-rate
compare with the death-rate?

A. They are lessening in
this band. That is according

to the best figures I can obtain.
Q. For about how many years

have they been lessening?
A. They have been lessening

pretty well all along.
What is the principal cause of this?

A. Tuberculosis, and the children
have influenza perhaps once or twice a year.

The death rate is largest among
the young children. Last year

there were seven births
and 10 deaths.

iv.
A beach?
A. Yes.

Q. Is that an old
Indian village?

A. Yes. It was old
when I was there in 1863.

Q. Were there any evidences
of occupation then?

A. Yes. I counted 4,000 Indians
at Skidegate then.

Now I don't think
there are 400.[9]

All that was learned
was learned

from super-natural beings.
How to burn and how to steam

was taught by super-natural
beings. House building and cedar

bending was taught
by super-natural beings.

How to be and not to be
what to eat and what not to eat.

All that was learned
was taught by super-natural beings.[10]

Look up.
Answer to the sky.

To the blue.
To a cloud.

To the mist and the sun.
To the moon, stars, and wind.

To a storm.
To the horizon.

Answer to.
The horizon.

Look east.
Answer to mountains.

To slate and to scree.
To snow, granite, and slides.

To tree-lines and alpine.
To rockface, to glacier.

Answer to.
Glaciers.

Look west.
Answer to the sea.

Answer to waves.
Answer to krill and to salt.

To wash and to foam.
To pull and undertow.

To drift.
To tide.

Answer to.
The tides.

Look down.
Answer to the ground.

To the soil
the mud and the muck.

The sand, pebbles gravel
stones and dirt.

To the loam.
To earth.

Answer to.
The earth.

\*

Started in 1978.
Lepas Bay.

Northeast tip
of the Islands.

Substance abuse.
Juvenile delinquency.

Family disruption.
Native[s] and

non-native[s]
set up a youth

project with guidance
from Haida Elders.[11]

Summer of
Grade 5. 1983.

Summer of
Grade 6. 1984.

Age ten.
Age eleven.

I am sent.
On a 'solo.'

Two days.
One night.

Alone.
Three matches.

One potato.
One small pot.

One knife.
My sleeping bag.

Alone. I see
the sky, waves.

Alone, I see
soil, roots, raven.

Alone, I feel
rain, deeply sad.

Alone, I stare
at the horizon.

I eat raw urchin
eggs. Fern roots

I have learned
taste like licorice.

Hunger suppressant.
Finding fresh water

is hard work. I learn
this. Know it always.

I have been taught
about Watchmen.

About those who
passed on being placed

in tree-top boxes.
Bones on the moss.

Quiet spirits we
must never touch.

10 years old.
Alone on a beach.

11 years old. Alone
at the edge of forest.

I hear landsounds
skysounds shoresounds.

Groundsounds.
Animalsounds.

Ghostsounds. Sounds
live inside me.

Songs of exhausted
hungry aloneness

live forever
inside me.

Early.
Solo.

In the meantime
a time that means

all the meanness
of time moving

in time filled with
wind, mean wind

timed to tides, wind tied
to time in tides, yet tethered

to that single slack tide
in slack time

the slack tide, a tiny
time of still tidal time

when waters are untethered
from time, unmoving

and still, tides with no time
no mean movement

perfectly still, unstressed
surface, neither high

nor low, in nor out
unwinded tide waveless

tension exhaled waiting
a wind, a windtime tidewind

meantime meantide
tidemean slacktime

in the slack tide
meantime.

There is no
beyond the pale.

No limits to
pale paleness, places

of the pale, a pale
face in place

a boundary, a beauty
that is only wan and pale

beyond which is
out of bounds

the pale faces
of us on ships

pale faced masks
not beyond the pale

pale sails and the pale
figurehead salt paled

in pale waves, faced
into the pale

pale of nothing
beyond the pale.

*

My mother. Kitchen with plywood
cupboards. Window over sink.

Wood shed. Sunlight. Car
rusting in the driveway.

Rated seven. Three days ago.
Chernobyl. Pripyat. CBC Radio.

Safety test. Vaporizing. Rupturing
Steam explosion. Core fire.

Radioactive. Nuclear cloud.
Seagulls. Kale in our garden.

Having just turned 13. I imagine
seeing something flitting across the sky.

Beyond the beautiful, the cloud
the wind beyond the beautiful

beyond the beautiful visible
clouds, the Ukraine cloud

the invisible cloud, the wind
beyond the cloud and the cloud

beyond the wind, an invisible
contaminated cloud, contained

cloud of travelling steam
clouded wind, invisible beyond

the beautiful, exposed
to exposure, wind and clouds

the doses carried by wind
as a cloud, small particulates

beyond the beautiful, inhaling
cloud carried by beautiful wind

a thyroid cloud a lung cloud
a cloud beyond the beautiful

invisible wind moving cloud
stream current fallout cloud

beyond the beautiful unseen
wind the cloud containment

uncontained cloud beyond
the beautiful cloud, contagion.

Say everything in three, three
times repeated, even if broken

up, said three times things
will be remembered. Take looking

at the stars, seeing how the stars
are seen, the ways we see the stars.

How stars tell stories, the maps
and stories held by stars, star

filled stories are best three times.
This way there is a star for each ear

and one left for the heart. Three
stars, a star for both listening

ears, a star for the feeling heart. Two
ear stars, one heart star. Or the way

the moon is three times told.
The white moon one telling, turned.

Turning moon, sideways moon
moon making shattered slivers

tell me moon in three. Or
the ocean, always reaching

to three. Two times in tide
then a third, is one of three.

The ocean close to shore
is ocean two, its third oceaness

everything beyond the horizon
ocean out of sight is ocean three.

Remember too the ocean calls salmon
and sandhill cranes, returning year

after year after year. Sandhill cranes
and salmon called for thousands

and thousands and thousands of years.
Salmon. Sandhill cranes. Jurassic calls

hearing ocean estuaries, nosing toward
stars and the moon, pulled, pulled, pulled.

Find the eggs of twelve cliff-dwelling
peregrines said the mother

to her eldest daughter. From those eggs
make twenty tiny cakes delicate as clouds

and fit for hawkers right around
the world, men with leather gloves

who might one day call you as a lover.
Then go gather every second oyster upon

the coast, picked alongside abalones
whose rainbow inside shells you must

paint in perfect likeness, trading
those paintings to fishermen

whose nets you must gather up upon
the highest tide of the year and, under

the fullest moon, mend those nets
with fiddleheads, scooping out first

all the silver salmon which you must
transform into golden coins the colour

of sunlight on saltwater, water you must first
learn to balance in your hands and then

turn quickly to ice made to taste of dew.
The dew must be soft as a fawn's ear

which you'll understand because you'll
have learned to hear like a deer

having skinned ten bucks in morning's
earliest hour. From those skins sew

twenty gowns, one for each delicate
cake baked from the eggs of cliff-dwelling

hawks. Each gown is to be tossed aside
for every lover who turns you down when

the tasks they've set prove impossible despite
every practice afforded by your mother.

Keep us safe from those
who want all we have.

Keep us safe from those who
covet shores and salmon

gold and pelts. Keep us safe.
Let morning light find

our eyes each morning.
Keep us safe. Keep us safe

from monsters and dying
men, keep us safe from pillage

and demise, from mines and nets
from plastics and punishment

from things of rot and madness.
Keep us safe. Let light find

our waking eyes each
morning. Keep us safe.

Keep us safe from
warmed up waters

from no more water
mothers, keep us safe.

There is Labret
Woman. Dead

Tree Island
Woman. Creek

Woman. Foam
Woman. Ten

nipples, line
thin eyes.

Supernatural
necks, resting.

Ice woman.
Flood. Woman.

Woman who Saw
the Ships Woman.

A man white as spit.
A man white as spit

in a dark wooden ship.
A man white as marrow.

A man white as marrow
standing in a tall black ship.

Men whiter than bone.
Men whiter than bone

on a wooden ship gone aground.
Men white as eagles' down.

Men white as eagles' down
coming from a black black ship.

A man white as moonsnails.
A man white as mushroom gills.

A man white as seal pups.
A man white as oyster pulp.

A wooden ship.
A black black ship.

A man white as ash.
A man white as sick.

On a queen's ship,
a great big black ship.

With men white as spit.
Men white with sick.

One section
of the Raven Story

and the other shorter
of the two stories

about the Copper
Salmon were contributed

by a none too intelligent
old man of the Cod-People.[12]

Lot of my future,
what I have yet to know.

HIV.
AIDS.

Coronaviruses.
SARS. COVID-19.

Taking the knee.
George Floyd.

You can't.
Breathe.

Lot of my future,
what I have yet to know.

The speckled monster                                    Whiteness
Pus, scar. Oct. 24 1880 Indian Agent                    Whiteness

Use all possible influences to prevent                  Whiteness
Indians in infected districts travelling                Whiteness

Indians not infected by disease                         Whiteness
From visiting those who are the latter                  Whiteness

Be kept isolated and if necessary guards                Whiteness
Appointed to prevent contamination                      Whiteness

Adopt the most                                          Whiteness
Energetic measures                                      Whiteness

Jan. 4 1886, Jan. 25 1889                               Whiteness
I regret to say, not succeeded                          Whiteness

Getting the whole of the Indians                        Whiteness
Vaccinated owning to the poor                           Whiteness

Vaccine is not reliable                                 Whiteness
Except when quite fresh                                 Whiteness

Indians being fully aware                               Whiteness
The deadly character of the disease                     Whiteness

Measles the worst fatal disease                         Whiteness
Among these Tribes of late years                        Whiteness

With regard to sanitary measures                        Whiteness
What I could by personal influence                      Whiteness

Sir, your obedient servant                              Whiteness
Acting Indian Superintendent, Victoria[13]              Whiteness

All faces are brighter
in the daylight, the sun

on starfish, the sun
on your sleeping face

brighter than you
falling asleep in night's

no light that is horizon's
edge, the sun rising

daylight on the faces
of whales, of dragonflies

of argillite animals
of ravens in cedar

totem poles, their faces
brighter too in daylight

the faces of compasses
of watches, both glint

flint sharp in daylight
directions on the face

of water, brighter too
almost like tears

winks and flashes on faces
of sailors looking seaward,

the west brighter still
in all conquering daylight.

It is a violence
to rename places

already named.
A violence to

insult stories
bigger than yourself.

Stories were related
by a young man

of the Cod-People.
Some of these are good.

His desire for peculiar
compensation was so strong

as to induce him to extend
details of several.[14]

Once my body
was a thought

beyond a thought not
a thought but a blink

in a milky blue eye
a breath like a salt flat

a crusted field
the sea left at low tide

a hardened crisp
a shimmer a grounded

cloud an idea gone
to swim and swimming

I became a fish
a kicking salty fish

attached to my mother's
blood my father's hand

against her belly so
I became and also am

the land he came from
land holding back

the sea, I am made
of herrings and cabbage

and people who map
and ship and dam

people who fence
the ocean and send

themselves afloat.
Before I swam

into the world
I was still all the ideas

before me, my mother
and my father

and their mothers
and fathers too

who also took land so
I am those horse hooves

over ground, I am guns
and I am scripts

and I am bricks
and I am whips

and I am pelts
and I am crops

and I am trains
and I am cloth

and I am lumber
and I am mills

and I am houses
and I am bought

on payment
and I am schools

and I am grocery
stores and I am flour

and I am roses
and I am ships

and trade and I am
copper and a bullet

and a book and I am
all that I pretend is not me

all that spreads out drying
on a salt flat in a milky

blue eye and the moment
I am born is not

a moment but all
that was born before

me so my birth
is a swimming

a bringing to this coastline
this low tide, low rise

a voice and footfall
over land and water

of everything that
leads me here.

Got the ebb, got the flow
got the rip roar undertow.

Got the fever, got the cough.
Got red tide, got a slide.

Got fire, shaking fire
got the scar, got the flint.

Got some hemlock poison
got a rotten mussel.

Got no pearls
got some cows.

Got a musket
got the rope.

Got pock marks
got the math.

Got some shallow
graves, got the fever.

Got a clear-cut
got the deep deep sea.

Got a straining net
got some whale gut.

Got the fever
got the spark.

Got disease
got the boils.

Got the letters
got the map.

Got a wingtip, got
busted seabird eggs.

Got the truck
got the gun.

Got the ship
got the pills.

Got the salmon.
Got the guts and the gills.

Got the fever
got some wild.

Got the ebb
got the flow.

In the name of my first name
is the name that was first

Sarai, which stood for
quarrelsome so became a new

name, to follow becoming the wife
of Abraham, mother of Isaac

and so also became
the name my mother

chose for me, my mother's
name stemming from seas

of bitterness and sorrow.
She named me but my father

spoke to his mother,
her name the feminine

of John and meaning that god
is gracious, my oma ungracious

about my mother's naming
of me, insisting I display Dutch

heritage first, so my father's
first name, divinely

touched in the birth
place of wine and women,

our last name locating
lions, of the lions, fighting

for the name, where
we are located.

My mother held sea
her own mother from fields

of wheat and dust, my mother's
mother married a soldier

flood fixer mapping man
born to my great grandfather

a man with a horse and gun
but her name, my granny's name

the English feminine of Henri
and meaning ruler of estates

married to my grandfather
the name of my grandfather

a compound name of determination
and protection, or sometimes helmet

so meaning a strong willed
warrior who, married to a ruler

of estates, had two sons, one
named for beloved, one

named for graciousness,
and a daughter, my mother

who bore her own two daughters
the other not me named

for a star, a princess, originally
Hadassah, who saved people

in exile, who went on to bring
a daughter into the world

whose name is happiness.
She who bring happiness

into the world, whose
middle name is the diminutive

of Charles, think again of Lot,
who will return to that name just

as all names return us to the naming
and that which is in a name, my own name.

We can
hurt each other.

Our first breath
startles us to sobbing.

I can
hurt you.

I could
hear you sob.

You can
hurt me.

Somewhere we
might breathe and sob

together. We can
hurt each other.

It was day light
dreaming it was day

light on the horizon land
thousands of days ago

creatures crying out
howling *Hail*

*Maria* from a scurvied
ship, the seasickness

greased reverends, water
poor their sails flagged

flags their grey squally
coastward heaving waves

stormy hove-to the ship
on swell, on swell in

fog with saint-singing
dreams swelling high

cross hopes tall trading
craft cedar canoe

met dreaming daylight
dreaming discovered

land a grey covering
no footing from sea

land but no landing
only swell swelling sea.

Kattssequeye
Kusgwai

Isla de Langara
Ya-Sit-Kun

Explorer Bay
Ah-Gan-Slung

St. Margaret Point
Cloak Bay

Lepas Bay
Ocean Shoal

Beal Cove
Jah

Kung-Cha
Rhodes Point

West-Point
Slung-Soas

Kate-Ah Island
Argonaut Plain

Lauder Point
Shicalslung

Ah-sets
Beresford Bay

Narchum-slung
Dog Ledge

Beehive Hill
Haines Creek

See-alun-hill
Djah-al

North Island
Kudgeeonants

Fury Bay
Ya-Kwoon

Lighthouse Slough
Sunday Reef

Lacy Island
Red Nose Bird Cliff

Thrumb Islet
Ah-Gans

Ta Village
Cloak Bay

Lord Bight
Dedall Kwoon

Cape Knox
Dedall Kwoon

Gatenby Rock
Carew Rock

Caswell Point
Kundals

Old Barnacles
Cun'ni

Seat Islet
Ellis Point

Mount Alpha
Hope Point

Dalton Point
Peril Bay

T'kil
Kwai-kans

Kutchems
Cave Creek

Wee-clow
Tian Bay

Thomas Rock
Tian Village

Tian Rock
White Village

Tian Islets
Steel Creek

Coates Creek
Alured Point

Queen Island
Pip Islets

Ogilvie Island
Bluff Bay

Chigoas Kwoon
Cloo-Whock

Flamingo Rock
Dog-salmon Creek

Barry Island
Dog-salmon Village

Squ'lu Village
Hippa Rocks

Notch Point
Hippa Island

Hippa Fangs
Skelu Bay

Hippa Point
Seal Point

Seal Island
Rennell Sound

Seal Inlet
Gospel Island

Gospel Point
Twin River

Yakoun Pass
Ells Rock

Ells Bay
Fame Point

Clapp Basin
Hunter Point

Sl'asit
Gudal Creek

Gagi Rock
Gudal Bay

Van Point
Marble Island

Dawson Harbour
Battle Island

Buck Point
Gold Harbour

Pay Bay
Lihou Island

Bland Point
Security Inlet

Mudge Inlet
Recovery Point

Una Point
Thorn Rock

Bottle Inlet
Kootenay Point

Tasu Head
Tasu Sound

Winter Village
Shearer Point

Crazy Creek
Ariel Rock

Wester Point
Wright Lake

Horn Rock
Sq'i'na

Tana Point
Marble Rock

Chaatl Village
Nesi

Moresby Island
Kaisun Village

Willie Island
Archer Point

Bone Point
Security Cove

Lena Lake
Colton Islet

Skaito
Hewlett Bay

Russ Lake
Portland Bay

Tasu Narrows
Gasi'ndas

Lomgon Bay
Winnifred Rocks

Two Mountain Bay
Blunt Point

Botany Inlet
Corlett Peninsula

Puffin Cover
Gowgaia Bay

Nangwai Rock
Goski Village

Hadjilta
Gowdas Village

Nagas Point
Flamingo Inlet

Klgadun Village
Xil Village

Anthony Island
Qadadjans

Ta'dasl Village
Sao'kun

Hecate Strait
Howe Bay

Rainy Islands
Lyman Point

Moore Head
Hornby Point

Catherine Point
Greatest Mountain

Jeffrey Island
Kincuttle Island

Samuel Rock
White Point

Sgi'lgi
Dji'tindjaos Village

Tcua
Gowdas Islands

Staki Bay
Sperm Bay

Chuga Village
Kaidjudal

Ninstints Point
Skang'wai Village

Qai'dju
Swa'na'I Village

Gray Rock
Skae Village

Gull Banks
Gull Point

Rose Harbour
Ki'lgi Village

Bold Rocks
Washington Rock

George Island
Rock Islet

Carpenter Bay
Raspberry Cove

In Inlet land, oh, have you heard
of Inlet land. Such scenes as lie

in Inlet land. The strong tides flow
in Inlet land. Awaiting him in Inlet

land. Foregathering in Inlet land.
Prepared to taste in Inlet land.

Along the shores in Inlet land.
The Sitka spruce in Inlet land.

Through rain and shine, in Inlet land.
And were at home in Inlet land.

The moonlight falls in Inlet land.
Salutes his mate in Inlet land.

Huge reefs stand guard in Inlet land.
That guard the peace in Inlet land.

The varied charms in Inlet land.
Let us grow fair in Inlet land.[15]

The Haida name for.
The name means.

*Kung* means dream town.
The Haida name for.

The Haida name for.
Was located at.

Long sand beach river.
The Haida name for.

*Koot* means eagle.
The name given by.

The Haida name for.
The name given by.

Named prior to.
Also written as.

The Haida name for.
Swampy Village.

The Haida also called it.
Moving Village.

Gambling Village.
After the Haida name.

Mouth of the Tide Village.
Spirit Mountain.

Mad-talking Village.
Red-cod-island Village.

Village-that-fishes-toward-the-south.
Village-on-a-point-always-smelling.

Songs-of-victory Village.
At one time.

It is said that when.
After the Haida name for.

The-straight-town-where-no-waves-come-ashore.
Chicken-hawk-town.

Face-of-the-ground.
Help-received-unexpectedly-town.

The-too-late-town.
Hair-seals-at-low-tide.

Always-looking-into-the-sea.
The Haida name for.

Sea-grass-town.
The name given by.

The Haida name for.
Flat-slope-town.

Also known as.
Sunshine-town.

Common-hat Village.
Wide-waters-flowing-rapidly-down Town.

The name given to.
Place-of-Stones.

Swamp-hollows or
Place-of-ditches.

Standing-water.
High-up-on-a-point.

Peoples-town.
The Haida name for.

Raven-creek Village.
Point-town Village.

Straight-white-spruce.
Also known as.

The-town-that-hides-itself.
The name given by the Haida.

See-was-kwoon.
White folks' cemetery (of New Masset).

Cross the waters.
Hold a cross to the water.

The crossing waters.
Waters crossed.

Surface tension.
Water crossing.

Breaking water.
Broken crossed waters.

Water breaking.
Water surface.

Crossing waters.
Water cross.

Surfacing water.
Watery cross.

Waters break water.
Crossing broken waters.

Crossed waters.
Cross water.

Holy cross.
Holy waters.

Waters crossed.
Surface. Tension.

A brig.
A corvette.

With men.
A sloop.

A frigate.
With men.

With pelts.
A vessel.

A ship.
With gold.

The *Columbia*.
With men.

The *Lady Washington*.
With men.

The *Eleanora*.
The *Union*.

The *Hancock*.
The *Hope*.

The *Solitude*.
The *Aransasu*.[16]

The *Josephine*.
The *William and Anne*.

The *Beaver*.
With pelts.

The *Jefferson*.
With pelts.

The *Vancouver*.
The *Una*.

The *Susan Sturgis*.
With gold.

The *Recovery*.
The *Eagle*.

With men.
With gold.

With pelts.
With men.

Virgin fur.
Cap.

Pelt.
Labret.

A type of
adze, toes.

After cloaks
inlet, for

King George
the *Queen Charlotte.*

Distinguish
this land

for his queen
otter, a fortune.

emphasized
appearance

speculated
movement

Margarita
genealogy

frontline
charlotte

magazine
antislave

ancestry
ancestry

scottish
portrait

descent
episode

claimed
mulatto

support
african

african
ramsay

queens
painter

alleged
claims

castro
valdes

mario
cocom

sousa
allan

trade
that[17]

charlotte otter charlotte
otter charlotte otter

charlotte
otter charlotte

otter charlotte
otter charlotte otter

charlotte otter charlotte
otter charlotte

otter charlotte otter
charlotte otter

charlotte otter
charlotte otter

charlotte otter
charlotte otter

charlotte otter
charlotte otter

charlotte otter
charlotte otter

charlotte otter charlotte otter charlotte
otter charlotte otter charlotte

otter
charlotte otter charlotte otter

charlotte otter charlotte
otter charlotte otter charlotte otter

charlotte otter charlotte otter charlotte
otter charlotte

Lot of my future,
what I have yet to know.

Autonomous sensory
meridian response.

A tingling downward
from the scalp.

Whispering women
screens and falling asleep.

Lot of my future,
what I have yet to know.

Your wife, said
the very old woman to

the much younger creature
with tool-cut fingernails

and small straight white teeth,
will be a very very beautiful wife.

A smart wife
who will stay

with you and
care for you.

Your wife will be a smooth skinned
broken branch and she will pleasure

you deeply, your own small bit of alder
tree wife. And your wife will be a starfish

and your stomachs will be fed and full
wandering tummies with your starfish wife.

Your wife will be a stone
heavy in your hand you

will hold your stone wife.
Your wife will be a salmon

in the belly of a seal and that seal
will float tumble in a wave

who will also be your wife your wave
wife teaching you how to break, crying.

You will marry moss and you will
marry sand and you will marry dogfish

and a killer whale will wed you and
a porpoise and a shrew will wed you too.

You will marry a single thimble berry
so red and ripe you will lose your mind

in her curved underside, sliding down
her stem you will meet your grass wife

your worm wife your spider wife your
wife the fly and then your wife the stream

who will swallow you up
giggling you over your gravel wife

you will marry dust and you will marry an ant
and you will marry red cedar yellow cedar

hemlock spruce and huckleberry too.
You will marry a bit of driftwood

her slivers will love you sharp you
will marry rain and mist together

they will soak you but you won't mind
knowing summer will marry you too.

A marten will bed you, wed you nipping
your nipples before two blind bats

take you, wed you too. You will marry
a daughter and a son, you will marry

slippery seaweeds, a limpet, a moth and
the shell of a clam who will carefully cup you.

You will marry a beautiful wife
a smart wife, a wife with a mind

and body all her own. She
will be your wife your

fine and beautiful wife of all time,
said the old old women, said

she to the creature who married a wife
a beautiful beautiful old woman wife.

Lot of my future,
what I have yet to know.

I have forgotten.
I loved you.

It's as if.
I never loved you.

Lot of my future,
what I have yet to know.

I am both gone
and been, been

and gone, my darling
darling by my side.

I am been and gone
your waters inside

me and by my side
my darling

darling spring waters
both gone and been

by my side inside
outside spring

been and gone.
Spring lady carried

across black sea
waters been and gone

gone and been
wave riding

inside out you
return, returning

back and forth
been and gone.

For if my darling
you drink spring

waters, St. Mary's
waters, you will

return, been but
never gone, going

to be been, gone
and returned, waters

calling home
the been and gone.

Mimic
awoke.

Mimic awoke
ricocheting, tufts

pinging mimicked heavy, quiet
mimicking light, mimicking

sound froth, faults
mimicked course bluffs, cloud

chemical mimicking dense
air mimicking water

wake to thick
till, silt mimics sand

red jib iron
ore magnetic mimicking

flaggy black limestone
skarn mimics

greenstone mimicking cliffs
cut bedded being begged

mimicry mimicked magnets
hornblende granitic vein claim

mimicking pyrite fill a mimic
layer, chalk-like prismatic

clam shell mimics moon
stung embryos mimicking graphite

mimicking silicone shaped stars
shored tides mimicking scatter shot

gases mimicking cells
mimicking sky

mimicking breath
mimic awoke.

\*

Family gossip.
My widowed granny.

Takes a married lover.
Who explains geology.

As the answer.
To life.

Gives my father.
Bulletin No. 54.

Printed to the Queen's.
Most Excellent Majesty.

The Queen Charlotte Islands.
Are at the western edge.

Of the continental shelf.
Sparsely populated.

Communities are really
industrial camps. Isolated.

Dionys. With regards.
Best, Atholl Sutherland Brown.

A few unusually
tender shrubs and trees.

A brief survey. 1964.
The Plant Research Institute.

A few gardens
with extensive displays.

A few standard varieties.
Hardy species.

A few annuals
and perennials.

Little potential. No
further efforts. Restricted.

A few small dangers.
What we bring.

Box elder. Norway maple.
Horse Chestnut. Birch.

Hawthorn. Vine maple.
Weeping willow. Organ maple.

Black cottonwood. Garry oak.
Flowering dogwood. Higan cherry.

Cascara. Japanese barberry.
Siberian Pearshrub. Flowering crabapples.

Rhododendron. French lilac.
Butterflybush. Honeysuckle.

One depauperate specimen of tulip
tree. Poor growth. Wet climate.[18]

Everything so close to dear, says the deer
says to me, she says tug me from my fur

dear, the ivory of my teeth, tugs molar
white saliva stained line like tide

sand damp and dark, her voice tugging dear voice
of deer silent crackle clicking of rain on dry

cedar bark, red the colour of dear
deer's fur with grey undercoat

underbrush of ash after a fire, plume
to eagle's down which is cloud

and also creamy insulation so fat
like pale billowing wave froth deer's

snout slick as soft slime on a salmon's
skin the song of dear deer, the song

that is no song, yet tugs unsung deer
a mite's palsy snip bite into her skin

back hoof reaching forward
the scratching that is a hemlock

branch shaken loose in wind
strawberry vines dune-close

grass fed feeding all her desires run
out blood alert ears hard as polypores

small island deer islands of bulleted
heart grazing, this dear unsung song

sung to me, tugging on islands dear down
in brown eyed waters, down deer, down.

At first the monster was a monster.
The monster had always been

a monster, even came up
from the dark and the light

of being a monster
before there was a monster.

Before the monster,
there was only monster.

Still, the monster
was also clam. Also halibut.

The hook used
to catch the halibut.

So monster was halibut
and halibut hook.

And halibut hook was made
of yew, which grew next to cedar.

So the monster was yew and cedar,
shaped into hook, which was shaped

like the sun's edge.
The sun is a hook,

the hook catches halibut,
which is monster.

Sun monster at the edge
of sun that is monster which is hook.

Sun and fish monster, hook monster,
monster that is sometimes abalone.

The sun is abalone too.
So sun and abalone and halibut

and hook and clam
and monster and all that is

also monster, they all sit together
upon a sharp edge,

and then they sink down
but then they also rise.

Again.
To monster.

Fish kiss here where fishes kiss fishy
kisses, a fish kissing place, kissing eyes

open to their kisses, their wrinkled fish eyes
unironed saggy fish eyes kissing love

they kiss with kissing breath gobbling
fish bits of floating mouths open kiss, shut

eating they kiss, salmon kissing
salmon kissing snapper scales

salmon and snapper kiss bullfish kiss
herring, fish eggs kissing kelp

the kelp kiss of fish, of rockcod kissing
lingcod kissing halibut, kissed neck ring

of the muscle fish, the fish bladder fish
fin kissed fish of coho kissed trout speckle

kissed gills of dogfish sandpaper skin
kissing fish oil kisses floating under

the sea, fishes kisses and waves, a dorsal
dipping kiss, swim kiss surface breaking

kiss, buttercod kiss red lip fish kiss surfing
kisses in fish cyclones schools twisty kiss

current kiss, underwater kiss, salty kiss
estuary kiss, creek kiss, hiss of kiss the fish

kissing fish, flounder kiss a fish tongue
kiss, tingling sharp spine kiss all

fishes, porpoise fish and dolphin fish
whale fish and shark fish

kissing fish, a fish blink kiss, blanket of fish
fast kiss, watery fish kissing fish place.

Plate 155. A Haida
Chief's Tomb at Yan.

The remains of the chief
rest in a niche cut

into the top
of the transverse beam.

This tomb is of unusual form
and must have been erected

at enormous cost to
the dead man's family.[19]

i.
Oh oracle.
Oh latch.

Oh cater.
Colt coral.

Oh alter.
Oh hero.

Oh arch.
Oh core.

Oh tale.
Oh tear.

Tear.
Oh trace.

ii.
Her alert trot.
Her ace.

Throe role.
Ratchet.

Ratchet her ha
her eh.

Each hale act.
Her let, her care.

iii.
Halter cheat.
A leach.

Torch her ear, her hat
her rattle rot role.

Tet a tet, rat a tat tat.
A chore.

iv.
Rotate her.
A clear clatter cotter.

Hot earth char    otter    orca.
Lace to roe. A heart. Her trace.

That throat-toe chortle. Lore.
Harlot. Tart. Coal era. Cloth.

The ache, later. Alone.
Heal heart, heal.

Etch each echo.
An oath.[20]

| | |
|---|---|
| Datsun | Short-Finned Pilot Whale |
| Fields | Sweet Laurel |
| | |
| Esso | Butter Clam |
| Minute Maid | Common Labrador Tea |
| | |
| Canada Dry | Limpet |
| PBS | Hooker's Willow |
| | |
| Lipton | Nootka Rose |
| Milton Bradley | Shrimp-worm |
| | |
| Nabob | Crowberry |
| Shell | Red Alder |
| | |
| Kool-Aid | Acorn Barnacle |
| Kodak | Mountain Ash |
| | |
| Maytag | Purple Whelk |
| Levi | Coastal Red Elder |
| | |
| Nike | Blue Mussel |
| Johnson & Johnson | Stick Currant |
| | |
| Ponds | Marten |
| Dad's | Cockle |
| | |
| Wrangler | Trailing Black Currant |
| Aylmer | Blue Whale |
| | |
| Ichiban | Club Moss |
| Lawn-Boy | Pacific Saskatoon |
| | |
| Fanta | Dusky Dolphin |
| Old Dutch | Bayberry |
| | |
| Sony | Northwestern Deer Mouse |
| K-tel | Rockfish |

| | |
|---|---|
| Dentyne | Pine |
| Pulse | Western Yew |
| | |
| Campbell's | Yellow Cedar |
| Dairyland | Fork-tailed Storm Petrel |
| | |
| Pringles | Bog Blueberry |
| Mattel | Black Oystercatcher |
| | |
| Ikeda | Sea star |
| Sony | Honeysuckle |
| | |
| Frigidaire | Little-neck Clam |
| Honda | Dogwood |
| | |
| Huskqvarna | Red Sea Urchin |
| Coke | Herring |
| | |
| Players | Red Huckleberry |
| Fancy Ass | Steller's Jay |
| | |
| Kraft | Common Snowberry |
| Ford | Sitka Alder |
| | |
| Maybelline | Saw-whet Owl |
| Maidenform | Sweet Gale |
| | |
| Scotch (Tape) | Oval-Leaved Blueberry |
| GWG | Black Cottonwood |
| | |
| Sealtest | Razor Clam |
| Estée Lauder | Mountain Hemlock |
| | |
| Toyota | Trumpeter Swans |
| Tide | Squid |
| | |
| Vidal Sassoon | Western Thimbleberry |
| Chevy | Saskatoon |

| | |
|---|---|
| John Deer | Fin Whale |
| Random House | Steller's Cassiope |
| | |
| Ivory | Threespine Stickleback |
| Sunlight | Copperbush |
| | |
| CoverGirl | Pacific Menziesia |
| CBC | Pink Salmon |
| | |
| Coffee Mate | California Mussel |
| General Foods | Juniper |
| | |
| Weetabix | Pelagic Cormorants |
| Nestlé | Pacific Willow |
| | |
| Mars | Alaskan Blueberry |
| NBC | Pacific Crab Apple |
| | |
| McLean's | Orca |
| Laura Secord | Highbush Cranberry |
| | |
| Energizer | Ancient Murrelet |
| Thermos | Fabaceae |
| | |
| SunRype | Pine Marten |
| Pac-Man | Ginseng |
| | |
| Swanson | Western Swamp Laurel |
| Sara Lee | Dungeness Crab |
| | |
| Harley Davidson | Gorse |
| Life | Harbour Porpoise |
| | |
| Downy | Sei Whale |
| Talbots | Western Hemlock |
| | |
| Robin Hood | Giant Pacific Octopus |
| WonderBra | Mountain Heather |

| | |
|---|---|
| Lee | Rainbow Trout |
| Aunt Jemima | Periwinkle Snail |
| | |
| Fruit of the Loom | Birch |
| Fresco | Chinook Salmon |
| | |
| Staedtler | Dolly Varden Trout |
| Pine-Sol | Net-leaved Willow |
| | |
| Tylenol | Yew |
| Scope | Sea Lion |
| | |
| Spam | Blue Huckleberry |
| Comet | Gooseberry |
| | |
| WD-40 | Crab Apple |
| Friskies | Sitka Spruce |
| | |
| L'Oréal | Dwarf Blueberry |
| Kodiak | Pine Grosbeak |
| | |
| Kiwi | Sooty Song Sparrow |
| Helly Hansen | Red Osier Dogwood |
| | |
| Alpo | Steller Sea Lions |
| Chevron | Rhinoceros Auklets |
| | |
| Oreo | Alaskan Blueberry |
| Dove | Sandhill Crane |
| | |
| Duracell | Scouler's Willow |
| Midol | Bog Rosemary |
| | |
| Aspirin | Peregrine Falcon |
| Fujifilm | Basking Shark |
| | |
| Whiskas | Black Hawthorn |
| Hawkins | Anemone |

| | |
|---|---|
| Crest | Wood Sandpiper |
| Bic | Scotch Broom |
| | |
| Zippo | Lodgepole Pine |
| Durex | Coho Salmon |
| | |
| ABC | Harbour Seal |
| Barbie | Salal |
| | |
| Pantene | Cutthroat Trout |
| Apple | Bald Eagle |
| | |
| Kellogg's | Pacific Willow |
| Five Alive | Emperor Goose |
| | |
| Mountain Dew | Bog Cranberry |
| Tampax | Mourning Dove |
| | |
| Polaroid | Halibut |
| Zodiac | Western Swamp Kalmia |
| | |
| Sears | Club-moss |
| Walkman | Merten's Cassiope |
| | |
| Aspirin | Dusky Shrew |
| Noxzema | Hardhack |
| | |
| Kotex | Pigeon Guillemot |
| Cabbage Patch | Salmonberry |
| | |
| Volkswagen | Minke Whales |
| Du Maurier | Kinnikinnick |
| | |
| Pop-Tarts | Weasel |
| Virgin | Twinberry Honeysuckle |
| | |
| Hasbro | Western Toad |
| Nivea | Hairy Woodpecker |

International
Dickies

Wonder Bread
Jell-O

Vogue
Sea Breeze

Q-Tips
Stanfields

Cream Mountain-heather
Sea Otter

Rusty Pacific Menziesia
Hawthorn

Little Brown Bat
Alpine-azalea

Devil's Club
Gooseberry

I eat sea urchin eggs.
I walk home.

I walk the dogs.
I cry.

I taste oolican grease.
I wash Mac'n' Blow Crummies.

I choose Cream Soda.
I have no idea the importance of Elders.

I am suspended.
I worry about pregnancy.

I buy Player's Light Filtered.
I stand by Bill Reid.

I kiss you.
I say 're-raser' instead of eraser.

I slice my hand.
I slice cedar kindling.

I jig for halibut.
I skin two deer.

I spray my hair.
I am best friends forever.

I shave my legs.
I fight with my parents.

I work at the museum.
I collate the *Queen Charlotte Observer*.

I walk for hours.
I slam a rock

They seagulls.
They fog.

They black bears.
They tannin.

They shorelines.
They geologies.

They puffins.
They bogs.

They Grey Whales.
They elderberries.

They tidal.
They porpoises.

They eagles.
They salal.

They ravens.
They spits.

They spruce.
They eruptions.

They mosquitoes.
They killer whales.

They sealions.
They salmonberry.

They ripple pool ripple.
They tannins.

They quartz.
They salmon.

into a salmon's skull.
They salmon.

I step over starfish.
I balance on driftwood.

They inlets.
They sand.

I cannot spell ghost.
I dig for razor clams.

They crayfish.
They moss.

I pick huckleberries.
I dress like a geisha for Halloween.

They springs.
They bullheads.

I collect crabs.
I misspell.

They hemlock.
They peregrines.

I menstruate.
I love the Sears Catalogue.

They sandhill cranes.
They basalt.

I clean a hotel room.
I discover Judy Blume.

They alder.
They muskeg.

I apply eyeliner.
I play dodge ball.

They salt.
They kelp.

I wear a Daffy Duck nightie.
I pierce my ears.

They so'westers.
They storming.

I learn *háw'aa*.
I learn *chinaay*.

They watered.
They reef.

I learn *nanaay*.
I eat Sweet Marie candy bars.

They char.
They lichened.

I smoke weed.
I break my ankle.

They estuary.
They abalone.

I get a retainer.
I learn about child abuse.

They razor-clams
They horizons.

I babysit.
I learn cursive handwriting.

I cringe at Tampax.
I sing "Like a Virgin."

I read *Sweet Valley High*.
I read *Nancy Drew*.

I vomit Silent Sam Vodka.
I am told to swallow.

I key-tighten roller-skates.
I crave sugar and tinned ham.

I hate my parents.
I hang a Michael Jackson poster.

I hitchhike.
I lose a beauty pageant.

I fail math.
I dance with David Suzuki.

I am frightened by mortuary poles.
I ocean-kayak.

I stand in a cave.
I grow.

They pebbling.
They coho.

They dollyvarden
They stickleback.

They ferns.
They chanterelles.

They slugs.
They herring.

They red-throated loon.
They waves.

They kelp.
They galed.

They clouds.
They rock.

They flycatcher.
They dragonfly.

They stone.
They seal.

They ice.
They islands.

Lot of my future,
what I have yet to know.

Fentanyl and death
of friends' children.

A second
marriage.

Becoming a poet.
Happiness like a lover.

Lot of my future,
what I have yet to know.

Be careful. Be careful        seaweed slips                    be careful.
Be careful. Be careful        with the cradle and the baby   be careful

Be careful. Be careful        because killer whales are the most powerful. Be careful.
Be careful. Be careful        of nests but also of snares.          Be careful.

Be careful. Be careful        when small birds lift off together.     Be careful.
Be careful. Be careful        your mother and father, your sister and son. Be careful.

Be careful. Be careful        to dry fish, to set out red meat, to flatten salal berries. Be
careful. Be careful. Be careful        also with other berries. And with leaves. Be

careful. Be careful. Be careful        you will always run fastest, but with care. Be
careful. Be careful. Be careful        with your caring breath, with your hands. Be

careful. Be careful. Be careful        when you dress the dead     be careful.
Be careful. Be careful        steamed cedar is so fragile     be careful.

\*

Also we have two dogs.
One black, one golden.

The black one is Duma.
The golden one is Tien.

After they die. We throw
their remains into the Pacific.

I see my
mother sob.

And the woman  was half stone
And the woman  had a face marked with stone

And the woman  was a woman made partly of stone
And the woman  rose from the salt and felt stone

And the woman  faced stone and breathed stone
And the woman  was a stone woman

And the woman  made stone of which she was made
And the woman  had a face made partly of stone

And the woman  had a jaw of stone
And the woman  had one eye of stone

And the woman  held stone in an arm made partly of stone
And the woman  looked and her look was stone

And the woman  cradled a baby who was a girl who would become stone too
And the woman  wept and she wept tears of stone

And the woman  was a stone woman
And the woman  dove down under water and met stone

And the woman  felt stone too
And the woman  and stone

And the woman  and stone
And the woman  and stone

And the woman  stone
And the woman  stone

And the woman  in stone
And the woman  and stone

And the woman  was stone
and woman and  the woman was stone woman

Lot of my future,
what I have yet to know.

Divorce.
My father's death.

Childlessness.
Fires, endless wildfires.

Carbon capture.
Wars on terror.

Lot of my future,
what I have yet to know.

Sir, I beg to present herewith.
Very respectfully, your obedient servant.

Sir, I have the honour to submit herewith.
I have the honour to be your obedient servant.

Sir, I have the honour to transmit herewith.
Respectfully.

Sir, I have the honour to submit herewith.
I have the honour to be, sir, your obedient servant.

To the glory of God in the extension of his kingdom.
Everywhere I remain yours faithfully.

We are thankful for the measure of success.
I desire to express my indebtedness.

We are grateful to.
We are in debt to.

Special thanks is extended to
the stenographic pool for their cheerful perseverance.[21]

*

My mother finds
finding work hard.

She is the Secretary Treasurer
for the Municipality of Port Clements.

Once a month on Thursday evening
she takes notes at a town hall meeting.

She is a member the Island
Protection Society – IPS.

She is IPS's only woman
member. Men expect her

to make their phone calls.
Sign cheques to anyone.

She takes St. John's
First Aid training.

Briefly becomes
a paramedic.

Attends to the kitchen knife
killing of a grandmother.

She is a substitute
teacher. Soon not

called in. Too
liberal. Too artsy.

\*

My father makes up a story.
All the black stones, wind blasted.

On the shore. At the tide line.
Are bears who jumped here.

From the mainland.
And missed.

He does not know
about a stone woman.

Inside bear a dream, bear
fat aside, bear blood aside

the twilight innards
to the side, milky way

bones and star solid
human knuckle hidden

a human digit, inside
bear a whistling wet

sea of cells, a galaxy
of guts, inside bear

beaches and hunters inside
bear the gallbladder sky

heart and shit and snot
and berry-bits and skunk

cabbage gore. Inside bear
dust, the doorway to a home

ferns and fragrances huffed
back an octopus found a salmon

found a found mushroom abalone
crust, the shell edge of men, midden

our houses our hands
our elbows and knees

our piss and breath
also inside bear's memory

deer and mice and shore
bird eggs, nests whole

an anus, testicles, sperm
storm fury fur a grandfather

sons of the future
transforming memory

of memories, entrails
inside bear's inside.

Be careful. Be careful      set your nets with care      be careful.
Be careful. Be careful      the seal skin is full, be careful with your breath      be

careful. Be careful      when you are sitting still, sit full of care      be careful.
Be careful. Be careful      to hold your caring      be careful.

Be careful. Be careful      of hooks and knives      be careful.
Be careful. Be careful      and know that everything floats, there is care.      Be

careful. Be careful. Be careful      on sand but also in water      be careful.
Be careful. Be careful      exercising care in your judgment, being caring. Be

careful. Be careful. Be careful      of tides. They will bring you wives. Be careful.
Be careful. Be careful      of too much rain. But also not enough.      Be careful.

Be careful. Be careful      when salmon escape or when they dive deeply. Be care-
ful. Be careful      of shells that seem to sharp or too soft.      Be careful.

Be careful. Be careful      sometimes the sky is grey and sometimes it is red. Be
careful. Be careful.      Salmon berries can be half ripe. Alder can look like a

child. Be careful. Be careful  of boats that carry unknown gifts.      Be careful.
Be careful. Be careful      because there are also tricks and feathers, be mindful

and exercise care.
Be careful.

\*

Every time we walk.
The dogs.

On the beach.
As a family.

Seals
bark.

\*

Flame tests.
Science Nine.

Phosphorus, my first
favourite, magnesium next.

Bright white-blue flame, cold.
Evolution is not

taught. The science
teacher, devoutly religious.

Have I been abused, he
asks. Pipette tube. Bunsen burner.

i.
Before rock: raven. Impossibly
more more black

than this natal stone, dropped, then aglow
first sedimentary mud muddy pebbles

understory embryonic pacific
ridge tectonic iron ore ochre flavour

not yet sweat but molecule rain cells
pool cloud sheared particle to silt

to thick green slush algae mineral
feathering rivulets amebic spirals

to notochord jawless storm
breathe   begin nitrogen

cycles uncurling oxygen sphere
congeal silicone meteorite aurora

salty froth some faint fossil scent
of invertebrate lichen spore fern

then bone such
calcium, such granite on horizon

sponges mollusks asterisk shaped
sea dawn with fish

creamy whales cooling fresh water
for cedar trees, for salal for

salmonberry for blue
breaking from the dark.

Rare crust dust pox
lichens, limestone cliffs

spray spruce rust chanterelles
and birds, red beak red circle eye

oystercatcher thrush
sandhill cranes in estuary grass

wingspan dance shore nests
tuffed murrelets in flight tuck

away two-day chicks flying far
to feed and high and west ice free

no glaciation smooth lake beds
pockets for sticklebacks, bullfrogs

everything airy as eagles' down
a morning that

is morning, more
mornings in moving moss, alive still.

ii.
So he, blackened born stone
tidal conceived, oh tide

withdraw withdrawal pull back
bracken coming in, warm sigh

wave with bashed hemlock
wind fall driftwood.

And she, opened beach, anemone
wet long full hold still

a cormorant's neck-length inside
make a blood cell blister

razor clams then guts bruised
as inside an abalone this birth

pulp squall, puffins, sky tossed wet sand
seaweed coast barnacled rock salt foam.

Fist small split shell knuckle
into mist, flint

inside the bear, a man, fur skin
teeth claw spine eye

orbit skull indent
archipelagos and knees, hair and surges

skinning caribou goshawk gone
missing saw-whet owl

all the transformation masks slip
milky dorsal fin waterfall climbing

trout, still, a black slick stone
a slick black stone, fingered smooth into flake

into knife into shale into mouth carved
into pole a streak where sea meets sky, a lid.

iii.
If I grew with fishing line shot through me
with transparent flashes, needles baskets

a hook and a hat a hand to lung
with gull parents fire orange spat

hinged beaks, we squabble over urchin
eggs over oil ambergris and agates

golden opposites of argillite-born
heart muscle saline

salmon daughter netted seal
blowhole quartz nests canoes

bellies hollowed, palms upturned
mouse woman in a long house

tapping on copper here another eagle
talons in clay, our house errors

erratics, wind wind wind in a cup
shipwrecked totem bent steamed bark

warm gulf stream
pitching down sliding scree debris

return to grey layers offer the world
do not break along bedding

planes leave fissile split
stay in your creek stay upper basin

alone stay home back
with peregrine-warmth home stone home.

Occasionally a boy comes
to rest his head

on my feet and the boy
who comes to rest

his head on my feet
looks toward the sky

his head resting on my feet
the boy sees my face

and while the boy rests
my face feels his resting

eyes looking skyward so
my face feels like the sky

my moon-skin white
pale milky way cloud light

eyes looking at the boy
resting his head on my feet

and occasionally the boy
moves his head skyward

resting on my knees when
I bend to sit with him

his cool face resting
on my knees or moving

upward and upward
so occasionally the boy

is resting his head
on my shoulder

and we look
each other

in the eyes
and resting sky.

*

After school is The Golden Spruce.
I only want white sugar.

Television. Trashy magazines. *Sassy*.
Years later *The New Yorker*.

Covers the butchery.
The Golden Spruce felled.

I am unable to
recall its exact hue.

*

About the time.
I begin to develop breasts.

I become obsessed with weight.
The heaviest objects in our house

hold. Our piano. A hide-a-bed. My parent's
king-sized bed. The car, cast-iron pots.

My father calls me
by the name of barging companies.

My footfalls are thick
heavy, commented upon.

Sometimes my mouth tastes of metal.
After I learn about copper.

Trade and war-canoes made
of single trees, the way cedar floats.

On August 15<sup>th</sup>, 2004.
Cutting and decision.

Rational refusing Husby.
Forest Products permits.

To harvest culturally.
Modified cedar trees.

The courts made clear.
It is the responsibility of the Haida.

To delineate clearly.
The Aboriginal right.

They assert.
Would be infringed.

*It appears clear the Haida.*
*Have occupied the Queen Charlotte Islands.*

*Since before 1846. And have been.*
*The only aboriginal people living.*

*On the Queen Charlotte Islands.*
*Since that time.*[22]

A separate word
for red cedar.

A separate word
for yellow cedar.

A separate word
for each tree's trunk

each tree's bough
each tree's outer bark

each tree's inner bark
each tree's roots

each tree's crown.
A separate word

for red cedar's
thick inner bark.

A verb that means
to go out harvesting bark

to pull inner bark
from outer bark

to take a bark board
to take a plank from a tree.

A verb that means
to fall a tree

to bend a board
to make a box

to weave
to carve

to bend the corners
of a bentwood box.

Cedar makes
words making cedar.

Cedar makes skirts
makes boxes and boats.

Cedar makes curved
knives carving

cedar frogs
cedar canoes.

Cedar makes separate
words making cedar.[23]

When you bleed you
will bleed uninjured

left uninjured by the sand
left uninjured by the shore

you will bleed uninjured
bleeding by the moss

bleeding below cedars
you will bleed uninjured

bleeding as you swim
left uninjured by the waves

bleeding as you walk
bleeding as you breathe

breathing in salal, breathing
and bleeding uninjured

you will breathe in salmon
and salmonberry too, you

will breathe and bleed
uninjured, uninjured by wind

uninjured by starfish
by catfish or bullfish

by bullkelp or crabs
by bear, deer, or mole

you will bleed uninjured
bleeding as you cry

bleeding as you ache
as you stumble and fall

as you call
out, as you wait

as you change
as you hate

as you write
you will bleed

bleeding uninjured
in the rain, in the wind

you will bleed
uninjured.

Lot of my future,
what I have yet to know.

Subsidence. Land
slowly sinking.

I will see Tokyo.
Live in Seoul.

I will dream
in other languages.

Hurricanes drown
cities. Global. Warming.

Lot of my future,
what I have yet to know.

*

My best friend came to work with me.
Actually, she is now dead.

We lived in a tent for two months.
Our sweat and condensation.

Pooled and mildewed.
Between our sleeping bags.

And the ground.
But every day.

We swam
in the ocean.

You may not kill the cedar bark;
you may not kill a salmon's skin.

You may not kill a fawn;
you may not kill the things that burn.

You may not kill an eel, an otter, or a seal.
You may not kill your foe.

You must never kill your love.
You may not kill a berry on a plant;

you must not kill a razor clam.
You must not kill a whale,

a snowy mountaintop, a balancing bit of drop,
or even two stray blades of grass on a forest floor.

You must not kill the spot where alders grow.
You must not kill the salt, the water,

the tide, or any bits of shore.
You must not kill a cod, a dogfish egg,

a baby bird or worst of all her nest. You may
not kill in anger; you may not kill in greed.

You must not kill in spite.
You must not kill a sapling yew.

You must not kill a shrew.
You may not kill a mouse, a mushroom, or the fog.

You must never kill a man
his sister, or his song.

\*

I dream of the light blue coat.
My older cousin wears it.

Thin nylon. Down filled. A 'puffer.'
It speaks *city* to me.

I want it badly.
The feel of something not here.

Long after elementary school.
I learn my cousin was sexually abused.

For many years.
By mum's brother.

My uncle.
He never visited.

The coat came
to me as a hand-me-down.

Modified Mercalli
Intensity Scale

i.
Not felt
except rarely.

Sometimes birds, animals
uneasy or disturbed.

Sometimes dizziness
or nausea.

Sometimes trees, structures
liquids, bodies of water

may sway, doors may
swing very slowly.

ii.
Weak. Felt indoors by few especially
sensitive, or nervous persons.

Sometimes hanging objects may swing
especially when delicately suspended.

Sometimes trees, structures
liquids, bodies of water

may sway, doors may
swing very slowly.

Sometimes birds, animals
uneasy or disturbed.

Sometimes dizziness
or nausea.

\*
Felt. Sway.
Very slowly.

Windows open.
Desks in tidy rows.

Animal.
Nausea.

iii.
Weak. Felt indoors by several
motion usually rapid vibration.

Sometimes not recognized
to be an earthquake.

Vibration like that due to passing of light
or lightly loaded trucks, or heavy

trucks some distance away. Hanging
objects may swing slightly.

Rocked standing
motor cars slightly.

\*
Felt indoors.
Rapid vibration.

Loaded.
Heavy.

I go to sleep.
I wake up.

I recall
a rape.

I was not.
Present.

Standing. Slightly.
Shifted. Hanging.

iv.
Light. Felt indoors by many
outdoors by few.

Awakened few
especially light sleepers.

Frightened no one unless
apprehensive from previous experience.

Vibration like passing of heavy
or heavily loaded trucks. Sensation

like heavy body striking building
or falling of heavy objects to inside.

Rattling of dishes, windows, doors
glassware and crockery clink and clash.

Creaking of walls, frame. Hanging
objects swing in numerous instances.

Disturbed liquids in open vessels slightly.
Rocked standing motor cars slightly.

v.
Moderate. Felt indoors by practically all
outdoors by many or most.

Awakened many, or most. Frightened few
slight excitement, a few ran outdoors.

Buildings trembled throughout. Broke
dishes, glassware, to some extent.

Cracked windows—in some cases
but not generally. Overturned

small or unstable objects. Hanging
objects, doors, swing generally or considerably.

Knocked pictures against walls
or swung them out of place.

Opened or closed, doors, shutters
abruptly. Pendulum clocks stopped

started, or ran fast, or slow. Moved
small objects, furnishings, the latter

to slight extent. Spilled liquids in small
amounts from well-filled

open containers.
Trees, bushes, shaken slightly.

*

Who does one.
Call?

Car seats.
Fields.

What site
not alarmed?

Spilled well-filled.
Open containers.

vi.
Strong. Felt by all
indoors and outdoors.

Frightened many, excitement
general, some alarm, many ran outdoors.

Awakened all. Persons made to move
unsteadily. Trees, bushes, shaken

slightly to moderately. Liquid set in strong
motion. Small bells rang—church, chapel, school.

Damage slight in poorly
built buildings. Fall

of plaster in small amount. Cracked
plaster somewhat, especially fine          .

cracks chimneys in some instances.
Broke dishes, glassware, in considerable

quantity, also some windows. Fall
of knick-knacks, books, pictures.

Overturned furniture, in many instances.
Moved furnishings of moderately heavy kind.

vii.
Very strong. Frightened all.
General alarm

all ran outdoors. Some
or many, found it difficult to stand.

Noticed by persons driving motor cars.
Trees and bushes shaken moderately to strongly.

Waves on ponds, lakes, and running water.
Water turbid from mud stirred up.

Incaving to some extent of sand or gravel stream banks.
Rang large church bells, etc. Suspended

objects made to quiver. Damage negligible
in buildings of good design and construction

slight to moderate in well-built ordinary buildings
considerable in poorly built or badly designed

buildings, abode houses, old walls (especially
where laid up without mortar), spires, etc.

Cracked chimneys to considerable extent
walls to some extent.

Fall of plaster in considerable to large
amount, also some stucco. Broke

numerous windows, furniture to some extent.
Shook down loosened brickwork and tiles.

Dislodged bricks and stones. Damage
considerable to concrete irrigation ditches.

*

Panic. In ditches.
The whales migrate.

I touch a war canoe. Cedar.
Cedar to ward off moths.

Cedar chips, mud.
Crushed into a t-shirt.

Incaving.
Difficult to stand.

viii.
Severe. Fright general
alarm approaches panic.

Disturbed persons
driving motor cars.

Trees shaken strongly—branches
trunks, broken off, especially palm trees.

Ejected sand and mud
in small amounts.

Changes: temporary, permanent
in flow of springs and wells

dry wells renewed flow
in temperature of spring and well waters.

Fall of walls.
Wet ground

to some extent also
ground on steep slopes.

Twisting, fall of chimneys, columns
monuments, also factory stack, towers.

Moved conspicuously
overturned, very heavy furniture.

\*

Fall. Of Walls.
Fall.

Twisting. Wet.
Ground.

Very heavy.
Overturned.

ix.
Violent. Panic general. Cracked
ground conspicuously.

Damage considerable.
Some collapse in large part

or wholly shifted frame
buildings off foundations

racked frames; serious to reservoirs
underground pipes sometimes broken.

x.
Extreme. Cracked ground
especially when loose and wet.

Fissures up to a yard in width
ran parallel to canal and stream banks.

Landslides. Shifted sand and mud horizontally.
Threw water on banks of canals, lakes, rivers.

Bent railroad rails slightly. Open cracks
broad wavy folds in pavements, asphalt.

Caused sea-waves. Bent railroad rails
greatly, and thrust them endwise.

Damage total. Landslides
falls of rock of significant character.

Wrenched loose, tore off, large rock masses.
Threw objects upward into the air.

\*

Bent. Woken.
Broken. Underground.[24]

Lot of my future,
what I have yet to know.

Herd.
Immunity.

Colony.
Collapse.

Range.
Shifts.

Lot of my future,
what I have yet to know.

Dear Chief _____.
Mr. _____, District Supervisor

informed us of the Band
Council Resolution concerning

harvesting of kelp on the shores
of the Queen Charlotte Islands.

I will, of course, bring this
to the Minister's attention

Yours sincerely
Special Assistant.[25]

\*

My sister is a sleepwalker.
Also, she is terrified.

Of tsunamis.
For two years.

She calls out before bed.
Mum! Dad!

Where will we go
after we have washed away?

We imagine disaster, hoping for kindness.
We look for that kindness. We imagine disaster.

We arrive at the earth, quake split and see
sea spit froth and balance, rock mush bullfrogs

and fog with starfish. In tide pools
that are not tributaries, we wait. We wade

wishing, imagine disaster.
We also fish. Fins are what we carve

crave, imagining disaster, the tsunamis that will
deliver docks and mounds, moles from ocean-

under, an unknowable global, warming, we wait,
fishing, lines cast tide-ward, the pull of abdomens,

sea abalone salal green our nets bobbing,
looking for kindness in the bears or wasps,

egg pollination we wait, sharkskin, imagine disaster.
We awake cranky, grumble but are kindred

with yew trees and ewes that are not trees,
the laurel and gorse and heather and alder.

All kindness to us, we imagine disaster,
walking in sand agate sunshine shipwrecked

cloud trout and also newts who try to speak,
a raven's beak, we hope for kindness.

Seaweed televisions, how walrus and sea-lions
have begun to Skype, the world is there, whales

are there, yelling is there the yip of blue, of orange
and white and brown. We are a stream

and the banks of a stream and gulls,
something sticky tricky, we imagine disaster.

We count and we learn. Still quaking warmth
millimetre by millimetre the stub of a log

spiky knot snag loud a quirky eagle leaf needle.
We also hold onto mushrooms in moss,

hoping for kindness rooted in coho's scales
and spring-salmon too, marching

toward the mainland now. Grey orchids our pillows
clutched because we did learn kindness,

and now we imagine disaster.
We are layered, chubby beetles war-torn

hemlock berries and longhouses abscessed
with our toothy dismissal. Even whittled cedar

is canoe-hate slipshod sideways
smacking down satellites and maps,

we imagine ourselves. Terrified white seaweed,
weed, a shell with no mollusk. Such ships

moon floating tugging we mistook
kindness, imagine disaster.

We search for fresh water.
Long lists lingcod willow songbird

a chainsaw of seals,
the layers of blubber

something like new butter like pirates.
We trade beads, copper plugs a volcano,

beach a dragonfly walking
leashed by a caddisfly ripple the dogs

join us too, our cats, our stuff stuffed
trunked tack, dry barrels, wool, sugar

and the flowering menziesia.
These are just the beginnings

of our catalogues, barnacles
black cottonwood with riffle

debris insects landing.
We also want to sing

with strings and clapping drums,
voices lift but also lie down

with our hearts we craft
jetliners gently, gentle now,

and steam with engines tea and say kindness,
kindness again, and imagine disaster.

We knowingly loved, hoping for kindness
on Twitter and after the holocaust,

with eyes fixed on pine orb drops of crab oil
highway trail automobiles to the stars

combustion halibut a Dolly Varden
electroshocker sampling on open fire pits,

bridges, we bring tents, the stench
of tuberculosis or a plague. Holding the eye,

the ovoid eye of beaver and mouse
and orca, something above our feet

we feel kindness but imagine disaster.
We say whenever they are illuminated

how ships are named for queens
not nearly as black as mining for stones,

argillite animals underneath, not spoken,
bottom of totem strong, our arrival,

we imagine disaster happy for kindness,
for waves, marriage, our children

and our children's children
with new tongues the taste of a balancing

rock packages, Fed Ex'ed friends waving,
plotting out anchors, planning

and planting fields and crops
from stern to bow new files and claims,

a resting colony, a nap of migrating birds
with our plastic pellets beak-throat lodged,

the world wide web, also with our hands
and those we hold dear, slipping,

we imagine disaster, hoping for kindness.
We imagine disaster. We hope for kindness.

# Notes

[1] From the Haida Heritage Centre at Kay Llnagaay.

[2] Adapted from the *Royal Commission on Indian Affairs for the Province of British Columbia: McKenna–McBride Agency Testimonies, Queen Charlotte Agency.* Masset, September 9, 1913. Pgs. 1–32.

[3] Adapted from *The Jesup North Pacific Expedition* (1908), Edited by Franz Boas, Written by John R. Swanton: Introduction. Pg. 273.

[4] This is a contested date. Some archival documents suggest Captin Cook would have made it to Haida Gwaii in 1778, having left England in 1776 and anchoring in Nootka Sound in 1778 before heading north to Alaska. In excerpts printed in the *Chamber's Journal* (March 30th, 1872) from *Queen Charlotte Islands: a narrative of discovery and adventure in the North Pacific* (1872), by Poole, F. London: Hurst and Blackett, the date given of Captin Cook's arrival on Haida Gwaii is 1776.

[5] Adapted from *Queen Charlotte Islands: a narrative of discovery and adventure in the North Pacific* (1872). By Poole, F. London: Hurst and Blackett.

[6] Adapted from "Britain's black queen: Will Meghan Markle really be the first mixed-race royal?" By DeNeen L. Brown. *The Washington Post*, November 27th, 2017. Accessed March 2018. https://www.washingtonpost.com/news/retropolis/wp/2017/11/27/britains-black-queen-will-meghan-markle-really-be-the-first-mixed-race-royal/.

[7] Adapted from the *Royal Commission on Indian Affairs for the Province of British Columbia: McKenna-McBride Agency Testimonies, Queen Charlotte Agency.* Masset, September 9, 1913. Pgs. 1–32.

[8] Adapted from *The Jesup North Pacific Expedition* (1908), Edited by Franz Boas, Written by John R. Swanton: Introduction. pg. 273.

[9] Adapted from the *Royal Commission on Indian Affairs for the Province of British Columbia: McKenna-McBride Agency Testimonies, Queen Charlotte Agency.* Skidegate, September 13, 1913. Pgs. 33–51.

[10] Adapted from "They learned everything from super-natural beings: talking with James Young, Skidegate, interview conducted by Gwaai - January 18, 2003." *Gwaii Laas* (2005). Pgs. 5–8. Accessed November 2019. http://www.haidanation.ca/wp-content/uploads/2019/01/jl_aug.05sm.pdf.

[11] With text from "Rediscovery.org" Accessed February 2021. https://rediscovery.org/?page_id=2

[12] Adapted from *The Jesup North Pacific Expedition* (1908), Edited by Franz Boas, Written by John R. Swanton: Introduction. pg. 273.

[13] With materials from Library and Archives Canada. MIKAN 2060525 REPORTS REGARDING THE OUTBREAK OF SMALLPOX WITHIN VARIOUS AGENCIES IN BRITISH COLUMBIA. 1888-1889. Accessed April 2020. http://www.collectionscanada.gc.ca/lac-bac/results/images?module=images&SortSpec=score+desc&Language=eng&ShowForm=hide&SearchIn_1=mikanNumber&SearchInText_1=2060525&Operator_1=AND&SearchIn_2=&SearchInText_2=&Operator_2=AND&SearchIn_3=&SearchInText_3=&Level=&MaterialDateOperator=after&MaterialDate=&DigitalImages=1&Source=&ResultCount=10.

[14] Adapted from *The Jesup North Pacific Expedition* (1908), Edited by Franz Boas, Written by John R. Swanton: Introduction. Pg. 273.

[15] Adapted from *Sitka spruce: songs of Queen Charlotte Islands*, Hatt, Daniel E. (1919).

[16] Referred to also as the *Aranzazu*.

[17] A 'snowball constraint' poem, based on Wikipedia entry: Charlotte of Mecklenburg-Strelitz.

[18] Adapted from *Flora of the Queen Charlotte Islands, Part 1: Systematics of the Vascular Plants*. James A. Calder & Roy L. Taylor. 1968. Canada Department of Agriculture.

[19] From *Edward S. Curtis: Portraits from North American Indian Life*. 1972. Tess Press/BBS Publishing Corporation, New York, NY.

[20] All words formed from letters found in "Charlotte."

[21] Adapted from historic reports to the colonial office and from late 20th-century government reports on flora and fauna of The Queen Charlotte Islands. See https://archive.org/search.php?query=Queen%20Charlotte.

[22] Adapted from "Decision Rationale Husby Forest Products: Cutting and Road Permit Applications Per 11, Lig 11, Lig 12 and Lig 12A May 11, 2004." *Gwaii Laas* (2005). Pgs. 19–23. Accessed November 2019. http://www.haidanation.ca/wp-content/uploads/2019/01/jl_aug.05sm.pdf.

[23] Adapted from "Words for Cedar and its Uses." *Gwaii Laas*, (2005). Pg. 40. Accessed February 2021. http://www.haidanation.ca/wp-content/uploads/2019/01/jl_aug.05sm.pdf.

[24] Adapted from *Natural Resources Canada*, "The Modified Mercalli (MM) Intensity Scale." Source: Wood, H.O., and F. Neumann, 1931. Modified Mercalli Intensity Scale of 1931. Bulletin of the Seismological Society of America, 21, 277–283. Accessed April 2017. http://earthquakescanada.nrcan.gc.ca/info-gen/scales-echelles/mercalli-en.php.

[25] From letter date-stamped March 10th, 1975, Office of Claims Negotiations.

# Acknowledgements

The genesis of this book is a 2013 conversation I had in Prince George, British Columbia, with poet and literary critic C.S. Giscombe. To say "thank you" would not do justice to my feelings of gratitude....

*Lot* would not have been possible without Kathleen E. Dalzell's two books: *The Queen Charlotte Islands Volume 1, 1774-1966* and *The Queen Charlotte Islands Book 2, Of Places and Names*. I am in dept to local settler historians for their unbelievably detailed documentations of coloniality unfolding in and across small scale geographies.

Huge thanks to Sari Dale, without whom *Lot* likely wouldn't have been finished. I sure appreciated your help! Thanks also to Nick Blomley for sending me copies of the McKenna/McBride Reports.

Sincerest appreciation to the archivists and librarians and statisticians who answered questions over the years *Lot* was written. Not all the research you assisted me with made it into the book, but your time is deeply appreciated nonetheless.

Excerpts from *Lot* have appeared in: *A Place More Void* (2021), Kingsbury, P., & Secor, A.J. (Eds.), University of Nebraska Press; and *Refugium: Poems for the Pacific* (2017), Blomer, Y. (Ed.), Caitlin Press.

## About the Author

PHOTO: BRIAR CRAIG

Author or editor of more than ten books, Sarah de Leeuw is a poet, essayist, and geographer who works in a faculty of medicine on issues of health humanities and the determinants of marginalized peoples' health. De Leeuw grew up in rural and northern BC, on Vancouver Island, Haida Gwaii (The Queen Charlotte Islands), and Terrace. She holds an appointment with The Royal Society of Canada's College of New Scholars, Artists and Scientists, has been a Fulbright Scholar, and is a Canada Research Chair (Humanities and Health Inequities); de Leeuw's writing has been honoured with a *Western Magazine* Gold Award, the Dorothy Livesay Poetry Prize, two CBC Literary Awards in creative non-fiction, and a short-listing for a Governor General's award in non-fiction. She divides her time between Lheidli T'enneh/Dakelh Territory (Prince George) and Syilx Territory (Okanagan Centre), BC.

## ABOUT THE AUTHORS

As the Board President of No Barriers USA, Tom Lillig has helped oversee its growth as a leading organization for unleashing human potential. A gifted storyteller who connects at the heart level, Tom has crafted groundbreaking campaigns for numerous global companies and organizations. Tom runs the Chicago office of Stone Ward, a creative agency dedicated to building good. He lives in the Chicago area with his wife, Cindy, and their three children, Coleman, Valentino, and Matia.

David Shurna has been the executive director, co-founder, visionary, and chief growth architect of No Barriers USA for the past decade. Building both organizational and corporate partnerships, Dave has guided No Barriers to historic levels of both impact and revenue. An innovative entrepreneur and seasoned educator, Dave has spent more than twenty years in the nonprofit sector. He lives in Colorado with his wife, Gina, and their two children, Clara and James.